T0157576

Love
Should Be a
TWO-WAY *Game*

Poems Written in the Deep Dark
of the Night

JIMALI MCKINNON

BALBOA
PRESS

A DIVISION OF HAY HOUSE

Balboa Press books may be ordered through booksellers or by contacting:

Balboa Press
A Division of Hay House
1663 Liberty Drive
Bloomington, IN 47403
www.balboapress.com.au
1 (877) 407-4847

Print information available on the last page.

ISBN: 978-1-5043-0679-9 (sc)
ISBN: 978-1-5043-0680-5 (e)

Balboa Press rev. date: 03/15/2017

To my loved ones—
My children, their children,
My husband and friends—
My thanks for your support.

To my medical advisers,
To GW and SP in particular -
I thank you for encouraging me
And giving me motivation.

To my peers at AllPoetry.com,
Supplying me with many a prompt,
I owe thanks also for valuable feedback
Given with the greatest of tact.

And to my publisher, Balboa,
Many thanks for your patience
As I struggled through illness
To deliver my work, finally.

I have left the best till last,
And this is an easy task—
I've always meant this book,
Which took so long to produce,
For a special person in my life
Amongst all the special ones:
My granddaughter, Sahara.

Sahara, this book is for you.
Remember: everything I can do,
You can do better.

Contents

Introduction

The poems in this book represent a selection written by me in the years 2005–2016, after I reluctantly retired from the workforce because of illness. Most of the poems were written in the middle of the night, when I could not sleep and I occupied my time trying to find ways of expressing my experiences to myself and others. The poems often reflect my personal thoughts, and from 2007, when I met my third husband, they also include love poems, which were expanded and used to develop the chapter "A Love Story", which is partly imaginary. My husband encouraged my writing and has always been very happy to receive love poems from me!

Later, I found a large poetry group on the Internet, (www.allpoetry. com) which uses peer review, costs nothing to join, and runs peer-judged competitions, and many of the poems in this selection have won a prize (a gold medal and some points, nothing of monetary value). Most of the poems reflect my experiences. There is no particular style of poetry writing that I prefer; this selection presents poems in free verse, rhyme, and a somewhere-in-between style, which is a mix of free verse and rhyme, and songs.

I hope you enjoy reading these poems as much as I enjoyed writing them.

OBSERVATIONS
AND
OTHER POEMS

I Lost a Word the Other Day

I lost a word the other day;
When I looked around, it had run away.
And yesterday when I was out,
Another found its way about.
There was I, feeling bereft and sad,
Wondering where my words had gone.
I didn't know the what and when
Or the who, the why, or the where,
But I knew that I had loved those words
And really searched around.

I've always loved the sound of words,
The shape and colour and feel,
The way that words sing out to me
From page and song and screen.
To lose the word is never nice,
And to have it happen twice
Left me wondering what I had done
And where my words had gone.

If I had watched with greater zeal,
Perhaps my words'd stayed,
And how I'll find them, I don't know;
So now I can only say,
With great dismay:
"I lost a word the other day."

Imagination

I have always found my imagination
To be the best of my companions,
And on the days when I have none,
My imagination is all I need
To get me through what needs to be done.
My best friend, the one I heed—
As imagination warns as well as praises
Every idea and thought that I raise—
It keeps me going when I am lost;
It is the one thing I'd hate to lose the most.

Nineteen Eighty Four

In Nineteen Forty Eight
It would have been hard to contemplate
That Nineteen Eighty Four
Would ever eventuate.

But it appears that in some ways,
Some of them hard to discern,
There has come the day
Where the book has taken its turn.

So Orwell was prescient:
Almost completely right-
All elements are now present
For the state to use its might.

Bit by bit, law by law,
The state has tightened its hold;
Strengthened and sharpened its claws,
Leaving me, for one, a trifle cold.

I shiver at the thought
This is coming too soon;
Of liberties so expensively bought
Being sold away for a boon.

Nighttime Poems

In the middle of the night,
My body may be still,
But nothing stops my mind,
And it does what it will.

Sometimes when I wake,
A poem will wander about,
Take a quick look, give a shout,
And wander out again.

I barely have time to see;
All this happens so fast
It always seems to me
That a wonderful poem has passed.

It may be that it's my dreams
From which these poems are born;
They are always so nice and rounded,
Always so fully formed.

But as is always the way
With nocturnal dreams and visions,
They go as quickly as they come,
And I rarely get to keep them!

The Goddess and Her Prince[1]

She stood on the balcony,
A goddess in white,
Looking for her prince.
He beckoned, and she began to descend
Elegantly, each step of her descent
Showing her tiny feet encased in glass slippers.
But then, as her prince stepped forward,
She fell, suddenly, falling and falling,
Each turn speeding her descent.
When he knelt to comfort her,
The guests gasped in horror:
As they watched, the glass slipper
On her twisted foot
Turned into a mouse
And scurried away.

---

[1] This poem was written for a contest on allpoetry.com to demonstrate the difference between the words 'fall' and 'descend'.

Wordsworth's Cloud

"I wandered lonely as a cloud ..."
Hang on, stop right there—
That can't be allowed!
Clouds are never alone;
Clouds travel in packs.
If one wanders away,
It soon scuttles back
To rejoin the pack
To form an ominous bank,
And if one breaks rank,
It is to form a brand-new mass
Of soft billows and gas.

So I pause when I hear
Wordsworth read aloud;
I have my doubts
About that cloud!
Because of this,
Each time I see
Those magic words,
I see a lonely cloud
Trailing behind the others.

---

[2] Note: The quoted first line and the reference to the cloud in the title come
from the poem known as "Daffodils" by William Wordsworth (1807).

Weird Photo Prompt

Every morning, eagerly,
I go to AllPoetry.com
To check on the new contests
Appearing overnight.

Sometimes I have a poem
Conceived the night before
That only needs a place to go—
Something that will fit.

And sometimes I need a prompt,
A suggestion to help me along;
My poem is there but needs a core
Or a step to start me off—

But I often come away dispirited:
Is it only me?
The picture and word suggestions
Have left me depressed and sad.

Other people's ideas of beauty
Aren't the same as mine—
The way it should be, of course,
But should they leave me so distrait?

Pictures appear to be ghoulish,
And word prompts are too personal;
And other prompts often cut
Too close to my own secret self.

I don't want to be depressed.
I don't like the sensation;
My early morning eagerness
Is tempered now with caution.

Looking at today's picture prompt
Has left me horrified;
I can only wonder at the thoughts
Of the creator's mind.

500 Internal Server Error

I heard someone say
The other day
There was a news report
About a man who shot
And killed a computer.
And the police were
Trying to apply
A charge of murder
To the hapless guy.

I jumped up with glee
And shouted, "I agree!"
It's bad enough getting a 404—
That's worth a kick or more!
But anyone getting a 500
Should not only be excused
And given an extra point or two
To calm his shattered nerves.

It's all very well
To say it's a trifle—
But I'd hate for anyone to stifle
My creative urge.

Colour

I was once asked a question
That left me bereft of reply:
"Do you dream in black or white,
Or do you dream in colour?"
To say I was speechless
Is to belittle my reaction.
How can I dream of a state
That hasn't been created?

The world is made of colour,
Not just everything
Sounds, letters, numbers—
Even thoughts have a glow!

My dreams are often memories
Of my daytime doings—
My actions, thoughts, fears, and longings—
And they are made in a coloured world.
Even the night has colour,
If only one stops and looks.
It is merely that colour is muted
When the sun is not on show.

When I finally replied, I said,
"How can one dream any other way?"

I Can't Stop

I go twirling, swirling
Up and up,
Turning, swirling, twisting, twirling
Up to the top.
I can't stop.
I go bending and rolling, roiling and boiling
Over and over
Up to the edge.
I go lifted and shifted, upwards and onwards
On and on
Up to the end.
I go up and on and over, up and on and over.
I go up to the top of the edge of the end . . .
And I stop.
It was only a dream.

I'm Simply Irresistible

I'm simply irresistible,
I know, because
My mirror told me so.
How can you not love me
Just like I love me?

I'm simply irresistible,
Handsome, brave, and debonair,
So handsome people stop and stare,
So brilliant the sun shines you know where.
If I had a job, I'd be a millionaire.

I'm the best man you'll ever find.
There's no one else like me.
You'll find I'm always very kind
To cats and tiny babies
And little old ladies.

I like to have you around me;
We look really great together.
You always look so pretty.
I'll not find anyone better.
They'll all be jealous of me.

I think you're very pretty
And you're very sexy.
Just don't talk about your PhD;
It doesn't look good for me.
My mates'll laugh at me, you know?

And always be careful what you wear.
I like you looking sexy.
Wear that red dress all the time;
It'll make my mates go spare.
I like them to know you're mine.

'Cause I'm simply irresistible.
I'm the best there is.
You won't find better than me.
There's only one of me;
My mother told me so.

A Metaphoric Euphoric Love Poem

I love you like
An Aussie man likes his beer—
With a strong head of froth.

My love for you is like
The attraction between
The light and the moth.

When you smile at me,
I feel as if I am a deer,
Dazzled by your headlights.

When I catch sight of you,
My heart beats fast,
Like a car in top gear.

When you hug me,
I feel enveloped like the cast
On my broken arm.

When you kiss me,
I feel as if bells ring,
Like my wake-up alarm.

And when you leave me,
I feel like crying all night,
But I never do—
I would look such a fright!

MEDICAL ADVENTURES

My Life Is a Predicament

My life is a predicament
Weighing on my shoulders,
Getting harder to continue
As I get older.

A wolf in the guise of
An autoimmune disease
Is working its way
As it pleases.

While my mind still sparks,
It is my body that's weak;
It is falling apart
As I speak.

I find I am imprisoned,
Unable to act without assistance,
Needing the kindness of others—
Or happenstance.

The ever-present pain
That continues to grow—
That can't be seen,
Buzzing in my brain.

Pain gnaws at my senses
And indicates loss of function
While I smile and pretend
That I want to be here.

So here is my predicament:
I don't want to be here—
But I made a commitment
To those I hold dear.

I desperately want to go—
To leave this unhappy life—
But I just don't know
How I can do it.

My Were and I

One day a long time ago now,
I was hijacked by a werewolf.
I couldn't make him go;
He wouldn't want to, would he?

We settled into life together,
Werewolf and I—
His name is Lupus, by the way.
At first, I sometimes forgot
He was there at all,
But there was quite a lot
For me to learn about Lupus.

At first, he just nibbled here and there.
I knew to take care
Not to upset him,
But as we both grew older,
He became hungrier, bolder—
His nibbles became bites,
And I decided to fight.

I fought Lupus with poison,
With toxins, with everything
And anything I could get.
And yet, still he survived.
So now he takes bites
And ignores werewolf rules
To stay out of sight.

The werewolf is a shape-shifter,
As is Lupus—
He changes from one thing
To another, always wandering
But always coming back,
As if he loves me.
But it is not love that drives his return—
His need for my soul burns
In his desire for me.

He plans to kill me, I realise.
He takes too much of me;
For now, we are locked together.
I can only ponder
The question of whether
Lupus will kill me quickly, kindly,
Or cruelly string it out.

Of course, Lupus doesn't know
I have a plan and I'll take care.
I'll know when it's time to go.
I have the means now—
I'm taking him with me.
I know the only way to kill a were.

The Ultimate Medical Exam

Usually, life's daily intimate chores
Are performed behind
Firmly closed doors:
Daily rituals well understood by all.

But when things go wrong
With the system,
The medics are called in
And set free to do some testing,

Which they do with glee, of course—
Cameras up bums, backless gowns,
Forced to drink thick white goo
Without a spoonful of sugar to help it go down.

But the ultimate in these types of tests
Is the dreaded ... proctogram,
The ultimate in entero exams,
To put fear in the hearts of the bravest man.

They make a mixture of potato flour
And insert it into you know where
(This, especially, is no pleasure)
And ask you to pass it at your leisure.

So? You say, no great matter,
Easy done, off I go, cut the chatter.
Ha-ha! Our medics chortle with glee.
This time, we want to see!

A proctogram is a great exam
If you like watching someone poo,
Especially when it's via X-ray
And saved for viewing on a rainy day!

Having babies is no fun—
Lots of blood, gore, and pain,
Considered to be the mostest
Of the grossest of these types of things.

But a proctogram takes the cake:
It manages to take a nice picture of you
Taking a poo,
Naked of all dignity.

I Have This Little Problem ...

I have this little problem
When I sit on the dunny:
My tummy just won't work—
And no, it's not funny!

I asked the medics what to do:
"You could try standing on your head
Or taking these green pills."
"But nothing works," I said.

And the medics just stood and murmured
And collectively shook their heads.
"There's nothing we can do for you—
You'll just have to burst," they said.

I thought upon my growing belly
And how to get rid of it all;
The creative juices finally won
As I sat in the toilet stall.

I stick a running hose up my bum
And rush to the dunny real quick;
"Just don't get in my way—
I'm moving at a double-quick run."

When friends talk about number twos,
I think of my little hose,
How I do my business my way—
Exactly how, nobody knows.

Congratulate Me!

My spine won't let me walk,
My arms don't like work much,
My shoulder was smashed last year—
I'm falling apart at the seams!

You can now congratulate me.
Today, I have graduated
From a scooter to a wheelchair:
A nice spiffy model with a little joystick.

My grandson loves this new toy—
Thinks it's the bee's knees
Of toys for little boys
Who have grandmas who let them play!

Of course, my new toy was costly—
Not just money, of course.
The anguish of the symbolism
Caused prolonged procrastination.

My loss of function and gain in pain
Have led to this imposition—
But within a week, I'll wonder
Why I demurred so long.

A wheelchair carries connotations
Of weakness, dependence, restriction;
But for me, it will mean freedom
To move around without help.

So congratulate me today
On receipt of my new toy—
Not only is my grandson happy,
But so am I, in a way.

How Will I Pull Up My Pants?

A wolf appeared to have caught me.
It didn't seem too bad to start—
It ate my flexor carpi radialis[3]
In a mighty screaming snap.

So, I thought, *That's that!*
The chance's remote
Of a repeat attack
Of such a rare event.

But then it appeared
On the other side, and leered—
It liked the taste of the other one
And was nibbling that one, the hide!

After that, I was suddenly weary.
I'll manage without, I'm sure,
But I'm left with an interesting query:
How *will* I pull up my pants?

(It's not really a wolf, I know,
And I'm sure it sounds lame,
But when I think of my enemy,
I like to know his name.)

---

[3] The flexor carpi radialis and the flexor digitorum superficialis are tendons of the wrist/hand. The hallux valgus is a bunion, commonly found on the big toe.

But there's more! Today,
To my despair, as I struggled
With my pants, my wolf sniggered.
I heard him move about.

He found a flexor digitorum superficialis.
Perhaps he likes it on a whim;
Maybe instead I could interest him
In a nice-sounding hallux valgus instead.

I googled *flexors* until my eyes bled.
I spoke to my advisors and said,
I asked them this: "Pray,
Why is there no wolf repellant spray?"

My advisors answered with a shrug and a pout;
They've never been able to work it out.
"So tell me, sirs, if you can,
How *will* I pull up my pants?"

The Saga of the iPad Attack

The other day, my iPad turned on me
And attacked me;
It jumped from my hand
And left a gash in my leg—

Clearly not a big event
In the greater scheme of life,
But the blood on the floor
Would be torture to any housewife.

The ambulance man was polite to me,
Puzzled why I called.
"No," he said, "no big deal.
Just treat it nicely; it'll heal."

But iPads don't attack every day—
And this one picked its mark;
My skin is frail, oedema bad.
Ulceration is barely kept at bay.

And as we know too well,
Ulcers are like unwelcome
Family visitors: they stay too long,
Fussy and untidy, never paying their way.

I treated my iPad warily
And took my gash to visit
A nice three-hour visit to the local—
The local emergency room.

The doctors were initially sceptical:
"Is this woman a nutter?"
But eventually, my co-morbidities
Convinced them to thread me a needle.

"Antibiotics? Nah ... relax, lady,
Don't make a fuss!
You don't need all those extras—
You're only making work for us!"

It was only the next day—
Off I went again, to visit.
The doctors sighed and muttered,
"This one again—what is it?"

"It's gone all red, a nice, bright angry red;
It needs help," I said,
And very reluctantly, they agreed
And wrote out a script at speed.

"Go away," they said. I went
But was back the next day,
Leg a mess, feverish, spent,
Lying on an ambulance tray.

"Oh dear, oh dear! Deary me!
What have you done to yourself?
Why didn't you come to us sooner?
Now you'll have to be our guest."

It's nice and quiet today
As I lie in my hospital bed,
A drip in my arm
And a very sore leg.

So be careful, boys and girls,
And be nice to your iPad.
You never know when it'll turn feral …
And turn on you and attack!

Hospital Stay

"Oh, come and get me out of here.
I've had enough," I say.
I think I'm going mad, I fear;
I don't much like the way
That life has shrunken in
To nurses waiting hand and foot
And the doctors visiting,
Making concerned looks.

I know I'm sick, but all I want
Is my own bed at night.
Let me go, and I'll be good
And try with all my might
To breathe when I am still,
To try to take all my pills,
And not to sit in the cold
In case I get a chill.

"Oh, come and get me out of here;
I've been here far too long."
I naturally put out my arm
When a nurse comes near.
I've begun to like the food;
It's started to look very nice.
The cooking here is rather good,
But I don't like their rice.

I'm sick enough I'd rather be
At home in bed with you;
I'm bored to tears with TV.
I'm sleeping enough for two.
I don't get many visitors:
My family is far too busy.
It may be that they only want
To not see me in misery.

"Oh, come and get me out of here.
I've had enough!" I scream.
Never mind the way I seem;
I can't bear it anymore.
Just come and take me home.
As much as I love this place,
And they love me, I'm sure,
I'm sick from being here.

Entering the Seventh Stage[4]

Like a novice entering a nunnery,
I'm going into a nursing home;
I'm not really old enough,
And I'm still inclined to roam.

I'm not waiting for God
Or close to death's door;
I am still compos mentis,
And I could stay for more.

My problem lies in my body:
It has betrayed me brutally.
I'm so dependent on others
There's no other option for me.

A chronic illness attacked
A long bad time ago;
The story is a very sad one—
A veritable tale of woe.

I'm fortunate to have family
Who are generous to me;
If not for their helping hands,
I don't know where I'd be.

---

[4] The title refers to Shakespeare's "All the World's a Stage" from *As You Like It*, Act II, Sc VII.

So now I sit in hospital,
My doctors appalled at the idea
That I might want to go home,
When I tried to make it clear.

Because I cannot manage alone—
That's when my accidents occur;
I wait and wait for a room in a home
But not without demur.

Because I'm only sixty-one years old,
And despite my disablement,
I certainly don't fit the mould
Of a nursing home resident.

I've given in to my doctors' demands;
They have my welfare at heart.
I'm waiting now, time on my hands ...
But that's how it'll be, from now on!

AN INTEREST IN TIME

Punctuality

I have always hated
To be late,
So I am always early,
Unless I'm late—
When I become quite distrait,
My mind all a whirl.
Like the White Rabbit,
I've developed the habit
Of saying, "Oh dear, oh dear!"
I've always found it crude,
Impolite, and rude
And always make it clear
The notion of time
Is easy to define:
Don't be late.

Time Comes to Take Us Away

A man stood on the hillside.
King of all, he surveyed,
But t'was of no matter:
Time came and took him away—
Oh, away!

People come, and people go;
Life goes on as always,
But yet, as we know,
Time conquers all as we decay—
Oh, hey!

Time has its companions:
The seasons, life, and death.
And with each and every breath,
Time and its friends carry us away—
Tick-tock tick-tay!

Time's companions dance
To the beat and the sway
Of the sound of the passing of time.
No matter, they try to change the way—
Ah, lack-a-day!

Time can't be changed;
Time can't be stopped;
Time has no remorse.
Time takes us all, come the day—
Oh, Time takes us all, come the day!

Where Does Time Go?

I do not count the minutes of the day
But am conscious of the ebb and flow of time.
I know my time is limited, and more so as I age,
But time goes so slowly now and so fast yesterday—
Where does it go?

I face an eternity of waiting for time to end,
For death to come and my time to cease;
For while I can count the time till my eventual end—
Three score and ten being the tally—
Old Man Time waits for no one.

The past is another country,
It is said, and it is so;
I do things differently now,
Thinking daily of the flux of time—
How much time do I have?[5]

My actions through my life
Follow me to my grave;
As I hope and fear that merit will tell
If I have achieved my best,
Only time will say.

I have my memories still
And those who remember me.
My children, my immortality,
My past and future together—
Therein lies the history of my time.

---

[5] This partial quote is taken from the first line of chapter I of L. P. Hartley's
    The Go-Between (London: Hamish Hamilton, 1953).

Time: A Cento[6] Poem based on Shakespeare's Sonnets

I have no time at all to spend
When I do count the clock that tells the time;
So do our minutes hasten to their end
Beyond all date to eternity—
Where wasteful time debateth with decay.
Make war upon this bloody tyrant, Time,
And threescore years would make the world away,
Time's thievish progress to eternity.
Pity me, then, and wish I were renewed
When I was certain over uncertainty,
Not wondering at the present nor the past.
Alas, why fearful of Time's tyranny?
Yet do thy worst, old Time, despite thy wrong
Against that time if ever that time come.

[6] A cento poem: a piece of writing, esp a poem, composed of quotations from other authors or poems. 17th century, literally: patchwork garment. Collins English Dictionary, *HarperCollins Publishers*

Heeding Time

Time can be measured,
Time can be treasured
By buying it with work
Or wasting it with talk;
By using it for good
Or wishing that it could.

If Time can fix all our woes,
We should learn how it goes—
How to stop Time or at least
Make it go slow.

But Time is an immutable beast,
And even Einstein didn't know
How to stop Time, or at least
How to nurture, how to grow
Our most precious resource,
For all of us are eventually forced
By merely viewing our reflection
To heed Time, without exception.

HOME AND THE LAND

The Cockatoo[7]

He came and sat on the fence,
Cocked an eye, and glared—
I thought, *What a menace,*
Coming and sitting there.
And then he flapped his wings and left,
His vivid yellow crest
Contrasting his white breast,
Leaving me strangely bereft.

---

[7] The spectacular sulphur-crested cockatoo, *Cacatua galerita*, is a protected bird in Australia but is also considered a pest. They will destroy the wood panelling on a home in a few days if they feel angry towards the household—for example, if they are refused food. Feeding them in suburbia is forbidden, as it encourages them to ask for food, which is not good for them.

Ghost Gums

I was surrounded by trees:
Great ghost gums
Planted fifty years ago
Along the footpath in rows.

As I lay in bed,
I loved to listen to the leaves:
The rustling amongst the trees
As if they were talking to me;

The pearly white ghosts
Bleeding pale brown tears,
A delight to the eye
As well as the ear;

Trunks tall and long,
Branches slim and strong,
Bending in the wind,
Swaying, dancing in the breeze;

Leaves a subtle green,
A green never elsewhere seen,
Not liked unless you've been
Amongst them all your life.

I have never understood
How anyone could
Not like the colours
Of gum trees.

I have left my old home now—
Leaving my trees reluctantly.
But my new home delights me—
Outside is a great ghost gum tree!

The Melbourne Cup, 2015

Every first Tuesday of November,
For as long as we can remember—
One hundred and fifty four years,
To be exact—
We have this horse race
That stops the nation.
Such a commotion—
More than 24 horses
Running over an interminable course!
Every contestant must qualify
By winning another cup,
And every one of them is examined
Minutely from hocks to withers up
As odds shorten and lengthen
And the odds-on favourite strengthens
As excitement builds for the Melbourne Cup.

The fillies in the stands strut and simper,
Dressed in their very best dresses
And wearing silly hats,
All the while whimpering
As their heels sink into the grass;
All the while gritting their teeth in pain
For wearing summer clothes in the cold and rain;
All while holding a tiny glass
Of the obligatory bubbly champers.

In every office and factory,
Usually full of industry,
No one's about; they're all out,
All tools down to watch the race
And drink a beer or cheap sparkling wine,
While the girls wear silly hats
And stand around and chat
And tell each other they don't know nothing
About the race; they've never placed
A bet in their life, while the office boy
Spends the day running down the lane
To place absurd bets on the favourite
At the local totalisator[8]—all part of the game!

And usually the favourite wins,
And everyone shrugs and grins
While my neighbour gives
A blow-by-blow description
Of his temporary gambling addiction.

But this year, something different
Came to shake the firmament
Of our comfortable tradition:
An outsider took the lead
At a hundred to one on
And won!

---

[8] Totalisator: the machine that records bets on a horse race (for example)
and works out odds, pays out winnings in proportion to the stake. Collins
English Dictionary, *HarperCollins Publishers*

A woman jockey riding in the cup—
(The jockey's a female—shock! horror!)
On a horse bought for nothing, too!
But she won, against the odds,
And this is what she said
In her impromptu victory speech:
"To those who doubted me,
Get stuffed, because women can do anything
And we can beat the world!"

I will always remember
This first Tuesday of November!

A Paean to Home

As I cross the river bridge,
I see the cockatoos
Perched in the gum trees
Up on the ridge.
I know now that soon,
I'll be home again.

Some dislike the birds;
I love to see the white of their flight
And the yellow of their crest;
There is music in the sound
Of their voices foraging for seeds,
Calling each other from dawn till night.

When I've been away,
I'm always pleased to be back;
The colours of the land hold sway
Over my heart, always there,
Despite any attractions
The rest of the world can offer.

I love the brilliant blue of the sky
And the colour of the trees—
That dull olive green
That cannot be described—
And I often wonder why
Anyone can call them ugly.

Even the drop bears seem friendly,
And snakes and spiders merely pests.
Even the heat of summer can be a delight.
And when our country exerts its might,
And fires and floods destroy
Whole towns and villages, gone
In a flash of rain and flood:
That's how it is at home.

Other places have their beauty,
But there is never a place
As beautiful as home.

I Dream

I dream:
I fly on wings made of spun cloud
Over the city, silently.
The wind makes no sound to my ears,
But I can feel it caressing my skin.
I am in a world that words cannot describe.
Soon it will be dawn,
And the world will awaken;
And my silent world
Will disappear in the bustle of life.

Drop Bears[9]

Drop bears are rarely seen,
Their habits mostly unknown,
Their lairs hidden from sight.
These creatures are cruel and nasty;
We only know where they've been,
Sharp teeth like sharks
And claws strong and big
From shredding tree bark.

Waiting for their victim, they perch in the trees
While the tourists wander unsuspectingly,
Stupid enough to wander about
At the edge of the campfire light,
When—woof!—a drop bear lands
From overhead with a blood-curdling growl—
And the result is a bloody mess,
An unspeakable sight, a cruel attack.

So, tourists, be warned of our native wildlife.
While you are told
There are no dangerous animals,
Always be on the lookout;
Always keep an eye open
For our unique, elusive,
And dangerous drop bear.

---

[9] My father would frighten us as children with stories of this vicious creature, *Thylarctos plummetus*, and the terrible fate that awaited those who ventured outdoors in the bush late at night, unprotected. For more information on these unique and mythical creatures, see https://en.m.wikipedia.org/wiki/Drop_bear.

My Land

In my country, my land,
It is different here: extreme,
A place apart, unique, special.
Yes, we have blue skies, green trees,
Flowers, grasses, and bees;
We also have spiders and snakes
And other nice nasties
Living together in great diversity.

A land of contrasts is my land—
A desert continent, an ancient place
With a history reaching back
Many thousands of years of occupation
In harmonious partnership, successful,
Symbiotic between flora and fauna.
Man is a relative latecomer
To its wide-open spaces.

My people have shared this land, our land,
For several thousand years now—
A short period in the history of this place—
Successfully sharing in its bounty,
Husbanding, nurturing its resources,
In partnership with the land, comfortable
Until just more than two hundred years ago,
When the invaders came.

The Tree

If only I were a great big tree,
I could watch with much glee
How life turns about my branches;
How everything would dance
To my coloured seasonal dress;
How I would be much blessed
With fruit so plump and fine,
Like jewels, not grapes, upon the vine.

To feel the bud grow in the spring,
To see the fruit the flowers bring,
To hear the birds nest and sing
And feed their fledglings on the wing,
To hear you eat fruit in my shade,
I would then be well paid.

The Fight

The cyclone warning was bland:
Cyclone Emma was expected to land
Before night.
We argued all day—
"Do we go, or do we stay
And fight?"
We stayed. We worked to clear
The lower levels of all our gear
With all our might;
But we gave up in dismay
When my shoes swam away.

Spring

I

Spring has sprung;
That's what is sung
In my family, anyhow.
The grass is riz[10] ...
Son, get out the mower;
Cut the grass, grab the blower.
Scrub the patio, get out the barbie,
And grab the mozzie spray.
I'll get the beer, if I may.
I wonder where the birdies is.
The kookaburras laugh
In the old gum trees,
So watch that their poop
Doesn't fall on me!

II

Camellia flowers litter the ground,
Wattle blooms yellow all around,
And the suburbs are spotted
With patches of mauve plots
As the jacaranda signal that
Spring has arrived: no doubt!
While a magpie calls for its mate,
Carolling from dawn till late,
Children cover their heads
With anything that may serve

---

[10] Riz: a colloquial word meaning 'risen', or 'grown'., and is taken from a ditty
that my father would sing at Springtime: "Spring has sprung/ The grass is
riz/ I wonder where/ The birdies is?"

To guard against the sudden swoop
Of a magpie guarding its brood
Of a single noisy black chick,
Its cries filling the springtime air.

III
Spring is signalled by light:
The time when day equals night
And the August winds cease.
But there is no peace
From nature's caprice;
One day, snow falls on spring flowers.
The next brings warm showers
That flood the droughted land.
As the bush grows drier,
The newspapers cry,
"Tinderbox! Fire! Fire!"
And the pretty TV weather girl
Points to the ominous whirls
Courtesy of global warming.

IV
Every season has its time,
Marked by counting the days,
Mostly predictable and certain;
It's always been that way.
But that is not how it is
In the Land That Time Forgot;
A season can be long or short
Or never happen at all ...

Spring marks the time between,
Celebrating a new beginning,
Marking the end of winter days,
Heralding the summer's heat,
And the segue along the way
May never happen at all.

PERSONAL REFLECTIONS

Dawn Breaking

The sky is a dull mauve with a blush of coral
Around the edges
As the pre-dawn breeze plays gently
At the tops of the trees.
I am awake early, unable to sleep,
A lot on my mind
Loading me down with what-ifs.
Each time I look up, the outline of the trees
Begins to deepen in definition,
And the sky begins to lighten.
The blush, more golden, melds seamlessly
With the now light blue sky;
And with it, my mind finds its way.
I begin slowly to see what to do;
As dawn breaks, so does my restlessness.
I am sure now.

My Son

I have a good son, indeed;
He always knows what I need.
He fixed the light the other day;
He said the wiring had frayed.
He's very handy with his tools;
He's smart; he's nobody's fool.
I only wish one day he'll meet
Someone to sweep him off his feet.

To My Granddaughter

When I look into your eyes,
I see myself look back.
When I hear your voice,
I hear your mother
When she was young.
When I see your walk,
I see my own mother
When she was younger.

But you are not us—
You are you.
And while what you do
Is a collection of our ways,
What you do and say
Is only you—purely you.

Be brave like my mother,
Be strong like your mother,
Be clever like me,
But always be you,

Because only you
Can be you.
There is only one
Who is only you:
Only you can be you.

To My Daughter, So Far Away

I walk with you
Day by day.
I watch over you
All the way.

I can't be with you always—
You are grown-up, I know.
Forty-one years ago,
You were a helpless parasite
On my maternal goodwill;
But how you have grown!
I couldn't imagine how well!
You've turned into a belle,
Confident and strong,
Better than me—
That is exactly how
It should be.

You did the work,
I take the credit—
Such a beautiful daughter!
How could I merit
Such good fortune
In having you here?

I still walk with you.
Every day, I hold your hand.
I watch you live your life—
Not vicarious, just exultant—
Watching you be mother and wife.

The day will come, one day,
That my spirit is all that remains;
But still I will watch over you—
All the way.

My Mother

My mother came to me one day
And asked me to google certain drugs:
Drugs that make one sleep
And drugs to make one stop breathing
If taken in large quantities.

I knew what this was for.
I had always known how she felt—
She alone owned her life.
As the TIAs[11] came more frequently,
We talked of her childhood.

And one day, too soon, she confirmed
I would be away for the weekend—
When was I coming home?
Sunday? "Good. If the curtains are closed,
You will know," she said.

I nodded. As I left for the weekend,
She walked me to the gate to close it—
As usual. "Ta-ta," I said.[12]
She responded, "Ta-ta,"
As usual. She closed the gate.

On Sunday, the curtains were closed.

VALE L.E.A. 1931–2014

---

[11] This is the abbreviation for "transient ischemic attacks."

[12] *Ta-ta* is Australian vernacular for "See you again" or "Goodbye." It originated as baby talk and is also used by family and close friends. It is not to be confused with *tah*, which is baby talk for "Thank you."

Kumquats

The kumquats have grown large,
Plump, and ripe;
But I am alone at night
When I eat them.

We used to pick kumquats together
When they had ripened,
Delighting in the change to the weather,
The end of the cold and the beginning of spring,
Looking forward to what the summer would bring.

Now you have gone, the kumquats
Are ready;
But you are far away now—
You are not here to help with the picking.
The warming sun shines on the golden kumquats,
And at night, the light of the moon
Reflects the roundness of the fruit.

Does the moon that sees my kumquats see you?
Can the moon tell me you are well?
The moon wanes, and Venus sparkles at her—
Do you see them too?

I've Fallen Off The End Of The World

I've fallen off the end of the world
To an unknown place
Without beginning or end,
Peopled by my memories,
Ghosts of all my regrets
And sentiments unsaid,
Jostling and shoving around me,
Attempting to engulf me
As I try to climb out,
As I scream and shout
For someone or something to let me out.

Naked Thoughts

I don't want to be—
I don't want to exist
Anymore.
I long to lie on the floor,
To not move at all,
To cease and desist.
Life is too hard,
Too painful, too difficult.
I just want to rest,
So let me go—
Let me be free;
Leave me to sleep forever.

Late-Night Musings

I think I might take up drugs,
Recreational, of course.
I take so many already,
So what if I take a few more illicit ones?

Or perhaps I could become an alcoholic;
That sounds like fun.
Drinkers always seem to be having fun,
While drug addicts just get sleepy.

I need a non-physical hobby.
Perhaps you know of one I might try?

I'm falling apart and losing the ability to do things
By myself, so I have been thinking ...

Plenty of time for thinking lately.

I am too much of a coward to kill myself just yet
(But perhaps there will come a time when I will).
A pity—it would have been an easy way out.
But I am left with a burdensome body,
With high maintenance costs,
Slowly disintegrating, ceasing to function—
As described in the specifications in the owner's manual.

So how can I pass the time till disintegration is complete?

My mind is not breaking down, at least not as fast—
Unfortunate.
Now is the time to wish for senility to start—
To start to forget, especially day-to-day things.
It would be nice to forget my circumstances,
To live in oblivion, not to remember anything.
I don't particularly want to live in my memories;
Most of them are not ones I want to recall at all.

The Deep Darkness of the Night

It is past midnight, and I cannot sleep.
There is deep darkness outside.
I can see the shadows of the trees
Outside the window, framed,
Outlined against a dark grey sky.
The air is still; the leaves are motionless,
And the scene through the window
Has the quietness that only night can bring.

I cannot sleep—a usual problem for me.
I often wake in the night several times,
And now I have stopped resenting
These episodes spent contemplating nothingness
And have come to enjoy the quiet solitude,
Luxuriating in the voluptuousness
Of the enveloping stillness of the darkness,
Almost reluctant to return to sleep.

I cannot sleep—a usual problem for me.
It is often pain that wakes me,
And I am forced to sit for a while
To allow the pain to dissipate
Enough to return to the sleep that causes the pain
That wakes me again and again
Throughout the long night—a long night
That used to be an ordeal to be endured.

There is deep darkness outside.
And as I wake again—a usual problem for me—
I lie and give myself up to the quietness
Of the darkness and the soft enveloping shadows.
I welcome this time now when I cannot sleep;
I lie and listen to the quiet of the night
And watch the leaves of the trees
Against the stillness of the dark grey sky.

Pedantry

I'm a pedant, a didactic pedant,
A know-it-all, a smart arse—
Ready and willing to expound
On any subject floating around.
You don't even need to ask;
I'll take up the task
Of giving you more
Than you need to know.

So don't get me started,
'Cause I'll never stop
Even if all you ask is
"How are you today?"

I Have Done Some Things Right

I have lived a life,
And when I look back,
I have been a dressmaker,
An actuary, an accountant,
An important executive,
A teacher, and a good one, too.

But mostly I have been a sister,
A daughter, an aunt, a friend,
And best of all—
A mother of two children.

Motherhood is my best effort.
My children are successful
And happy, well adjusted—
Better than I was and am.
I must have done something right.

But I failed somewhere,
Something most important
To anyone's life and well-being:
I've messed up my own life.
Big time.

I've had a few lovers over the years—
But I had to go and marry them:
Three of them altogether.
You'd think I would have learnt by now
That "good enough" is not really good enough.

So here I am now, alone and, yes, lonely,
Reflecting on the mistakes I've made;
I've never ever found that special someone,
Not even married to someone else.
It seems my mythical soulmate doesn't exist.

When Sleep Eludes Me

When sleep eludes me—
That nightly opiate,
That half-life of darkness
Where shadows blur reality,
When the air feels heavy
With everyone's dreams—
Where can I go but inwards
And curse my soul for caring?

My heart aches with longing
To be in that world of Sans Souci,
Where dreams transcend
That harsh reality of days—
The reality of pain and despair,
Of no beginning and no end—
To this amaranthine need to bear
The weight of this unhappy life.

Oh, to dream of a life free of burden,
Not to endure the weariness of life,
Where my soul flies free of care;
To cast off worry and strife,
While my body clings to earth
Bound by ties too many to count
That chain me by death and birth
To the pain of continual existence.

If only the night could bring solace,
Perhaps some dream could transport me
To the time before time,
To the dream time of my forebears.
I could dream I dance and prance,
Be a proud brolga[13] with black-tipped wings,
Flying free of my earthly bounds,
And share in heaven's surround.

---

[13] Brolga: a regal, long-legged crane, *Grus rubicunda*, grey and silver plumage, these birds are beautiful dancers, famous for their elaborate performances which appear to be both for pleasure and courtship. The Aboriginal people have immortalised their graceful steps through dance. I was assigned to the brolga by my father when I was born.

A LOVE STORY

You're Everything to Me

I was in despair—
Alone, no one to care,
No lover, not a wife,
Not having a life.

Then you came along—
Gentle and strong,
Patient and quiet—
Wooing me right.

I bloom in your love—
Like a flower with the sun above,
I open my petals to your light;
My heart melts at your sight.

Now I love you dearly—
To think that I nearly
Didn't want to see
How you could be.

Oh, how I love you!
Oh, how I need you!
Can you not see
You're everything to me?

You Have Cast a Spell over Me

There is no need for your spells;
There is no need to bewitch me.
That first day, it was easy to tell
That I would find it hard
To stay away from you.
Indeed, it is difficult to part.
I hate to send you away,
But I must be strong.
I cannot allow you to stay—
Even now you stay too long.

The times we are apart,
Your smile stays in my mind,
Drawing me closer to you,
Making me fonder all the while.

Should I regret our meeting?
I am in too deep already;
The time we are together is fleeting.
I want more of you for me—
There is no need for your spells,
No need to beguile;
Surely you can tell
You had me at that first smile.

I Love It When: A Song

I love it when
You look at me that way;
I'm loved like that—
I love you back.

I love it when
You laugh at me that way;
I long to know
How I can keep it so.

I love it when
You kiss me like that;
I want to keep
Kisses long and deep.

I love it when
You write to me;
I like to hear
Of how you want me near.

I love it when
You call me *love*;
I know you love me.
That I can see.

I've Become Addicted to You: A Song

I've become addicted to you—
I love all that you do.
I want to be with you
Every moment of the day.

I've become addicted to you—
Every word, every look, every touch
Leaves me wanting you more.
I want you so much.

I've become addicted to you—
I hate to be apart from you.
I count the minutes and hours
Until I'm with you again.

I've become addicted to you—
It wasn't meant to be like this.
I was meant to have a taste,
Not get addicted to you.

I've become addicted to you—
Your body I love to touch.
Your mind I love to explore,
A drug I can't resist.

I've become addicted to you—
I love all that you do.
I want to be with you
Every moment of the day.

I've become addicted to you—
I know you feel the same.
And this addiction is one
I never want to break.

When I Think of You

When I think of you,
My spirit soars;
My life brightens;
My love is yours.

When I see you,
My day is complete;
My joy is boundless,
My soul replete.

When I leave you,
I look for the time
We are together;
You are again mine.

Give Me Your Hand

Give me your hand,
And I'll give you mine.
We'll face the world
Forever entwined.

Give me your heart,
And I'll give you mine.
And so a part of me
Will be forever thine.

Give me your love,
And I'll give you mine.
I'll forever be with you
Always in my mind.

Give me your life,
And I'll give you mine.
We'll always be together
Forever in time.

My Foolish Heart

My foolish heart
Betrays me
Each time you're near,
Each time we part.

My foolish heart
Beats when you smile,
Flops when we kiss;
It won't be told.

My foolish heart
Loves when I gainsay.
It won't be told,
"Never love again."

My foolish heart,
Despite my wish,
Despite my mind,
Loves you yet.

Till Death Do Us Part

Till death do us part,
You will have my heart.
But more than that, my love,
When the heavens above
Swallow the earth below,
When the sun shines as it snows,
And the rivers' waters run dry —
Even then I will cry:
"Though death do us part,
You will always have my heart".

Loving You

You sit beside me as I rest
Reading quietly;
But would you at my bequest
Come and lie with me?
I can feel you sitting there,
And all I can think about,
The only thing about which I care,
Is to turn to you and shout
For you to come and love me.
My body tingles with desire
For you, your body, your strength,
And how you will aspire
To pleasure me in a length
Of time so short and so endless
That I float in pleasure
At each touch of your caress,
Exploding with the longing
To completely envelop you
And to keep you going
With what I, in return, will do.

Missing You

When I am not with you,
My heart trembles
With grief,
Like the dew
Poised on a leaf.

When I am not with you,
My tears flow
Like the dew
Shaken from the flower
At sunrise.

When I am not with you,
My soul cries out
Like a flower
Without water
In a vase.

When I am not with you,
My mind remembers
Your smell,
Like the scent
Of a flower.

When I am not with you,
My soul cries,
Tears falling
Like rain—
Missing you.

Do You Love Me Because?

Do you love me
Because I love you?
Love songs suggest it's true;
But I say nay.
I would prefer
It were the other way:
That you love me
While I love you!

Where Will I Meet You?

Where will I meet you?
In the middle,
Where lovers are supposed to meet?
Is there any other way; do you know?
We argue over stupid things
And can't agree on the major items
Of people sharing lives.
Lovers are supposed to have
A meeting of their minds—
But it must be on common ground,
Or else one of us must work too hard.
How can that be fair?

Let's meet here in the middle;
It looks like a nice comfy spot.
It even has the give and take,
Some room to negotiate,
A dance floor and a skating rink—
What do you think?

If we are to make a go of it,
We need to get things clear:
No disagreement over silly things
And clarity where it's needed,
But no quibbling over those stupid things
When neither of us really cares.
If we can heed these simple rules,
It's a date, right here, right now.

I Loved You Once

I loved you once,
And you loved me.

Where has he gone,
The man I used to love?
Your smile is wonderful but never for me;
Your smile is kept for others.
For me, you never bother.
Your words can be sweet,
But for me, they are bitter,
Designed to hurt me, to hit.
Your touch is electric,
But you save it miserly,
Just like your love for those times
When you need me most.
What is the cost
Of your attention?

Never good enough, never bright enough, never satisfied;
Discontented with what you used to like;
Always stricturing, demanding, commanding—
What can I do but retreat into silence?

A lover who doesn't love,
A husband who doesn't cherish,
A carer who doesn't care—
One who disdains to give affection
Or even to take it.

Never saying please, thank you, or sorry
To admit fault, like giving away your life,
Full of conspiracy theories
But unable to see your own corruption—
Where is the man I used to love?

Hold On

Hold on, take care, be nice,
Be careful what you say.
Take time to think twice—
Give every word its due.

What can you do
With a man who
Takes exception
To every suggestion?

Broken Leaves

Autumn leaves crush in my hand
As you have crushed my heart;
The broken leaves drift away,
But your harsh words stay:
How could you be so cruel?

My Song to You

You say that you are sorry,
You have treated me bad.
It's much too late now—
Oh, how you make me sad.

You hide behind that bravado;
I can't see the real you at all.
How can you say you love me
When you are hiding from me?

You say that you need me
All while you push me away.
You say there's no one more important:
But you never show me that.

You always put me down;
Then you call me a friend.
Why don't I just call an end
And you can cease to pretend?

Go sing your song to another;
I am finished with you.
Go and hide from someone else,
And sing this song to her.

Burning Bridges

So again, I incur your displeasure,
Which I do merely by existing, it seems—
Doing those things I've done before
And will do again,
Necessary to my well-being;
An important issue, you will agree,
Given its fragility
But which appears to be anathema
To your very *raison d'etre*,
Which, of course, begs the question
"Why do you stay?"

It's WYSIWYG, my dear: an acronym
For "What you see is what you get."
And surely, after all these years—
We've spent so much time together—
We should know each other by now;
Know the where, the why, and the how
Of each other's thoughts.
Surely by now, you would know
How it's going to go:
I say something to which you object.
Just what do you expect?

That I would let you trample all over my words
As if they are made of dirt?
No, I am not the little woman,
Subservient, submissive, deferential.
I have a mind of my own
Dependent upon no one
But myself—
So why do you bother?

And so you throw a tantrum,
A real dummy spit,
A self-indulgent demonstration,
A supposed remonstration—
Of what, I'm not quite sure—
To make me reconsider
What you knew I would do anyway,
Or just let me know how angry you are,
A passive-aggressive performance
Meant to illustrate your displeasure.
Isn't that so?

But you already know that nothing will change,
And as your tantrum, your non-verbal scream of abuse,
Proceeds and grows more irrecoverable,
Perhaps you will consider the bridges you're burning
As you go—no, I won't follow you.
But you won't be able to retrieve the situation
If you burn too many bridges,
Will you?

Crying Wolf

Do you know the story
Of the boy who cried wolf?
A story with a lesson to tell,
Including a moral as well—
One that you should heed.

To bluff and threaten and not carry through,
To not do the thing you said you'd do,
Time and time, over again and again,
Leads me to deliberate
That when you whinge and complain,
I can just ignore you; the problem melts away.

You've cried wolf too often now;
If the wolf came to be
And your threat eventuated,
I would surely be definitely,
Completely discombobulated.

Love Should Be a Two-Way Game

Gladly I will go to the gates of hell
And back again, if you so wish,
But think, my love, before you agree—
It may not be as simple as this.

The road to hell is paved with glass.
Wouldn't you rather I walked on grass?
The gates of hell are far away.
Wouldn't you rather I stay?
I would be gone for some time.
Wouldn't you rather be by my side?
But should I need to go so far or so long
Just to keep you here where you belong?

Love should be a two-way game,
With no balancing of guilt or blame—
So when we walk side by side,
There is no need to keep in step.
Just don't ask me to provide
Evidence of promises kept.
When has love been so solidly a thing
That I need to prove my loving you?

Love Clichéd: An Almost Cento Poem[14]

I am a sorry sight—
A laughing stock,
One who loved not wisely
But too well.

The course of true love
Never did run smooth.
I am sick at heart.
Jealousy is the green-eyed monster,
An ill wind that blows, no man, no good.
But love is blind.

In a better world than this,
As good luck would have it,
All's well that ends well—
But not always.

It is better to have loved and lost
Than never to have loved at all
But not for me.

---

[14] My thanks to Shakespeare for the well-worn clichés for this almost cento.

With Silence and Tears

With silence and tears, I left;[15]
Weeping I left you, bereft.
I remember when we met—
Oh, how could I forget?
You were so kind, so loving.
Now you are cold, uncaring.
You want me to stay, you plead,
You ask me to unbend, to yield;
I cannot after all that's occurred.
All the while, you demurred.
You call me *cruel*, after all you've said.
You watched as my heart bled.
As I wept, you just stood by.
Now I am leaving; you are asking, "Why?"

---

[15] This line uses the last line of the poem "When We Two Parted" by George
Gordon Byron

How to Throw a Tantrum (for Grown-Ups)

First, wake up in a bad mood
And refuse any offers of food.
Let your blood-sugar level reduce;
Then find the perfect excuse.

You'll need to pick a fight,
But don't make it too light—
A sulk is sufficient for little things.
Keep important things for tanty throwing.

Pick your fight, and make it loud
So even your grandkids'd be proud.
Argue and whinge, bicker and whine,
Build to a crescendo; it'll take time.

Once you've said all you can say,
Finish abruptly, call it a day,
Put your mouth in a pout,
Look cranky, and really put out.

Find a spot to pass the time,
One where others will keep you in mind.
You want them to know what you're doing;
Otherwise, why bother with tanty throwing?

You mustn't speak a word at all;
You must keep them all in thrall.
They mustn't know what you intend;
You must punish their impudence.

Rebuff all pleas for conversation,
Or even for compensation.
Refuse offers of nourishment;
There must be complete chastisement.

Once you've finished your reading,
Watched a movie or rubbishy TV,
Had a nap and called a friend,
Now's the time to call for an end.

Tanty's finished, all is done—
You've had your say and won.
It's been a tiring day, once all's said;
So dinner, bath, and off to bed.

I've Made My Bed

I've made my bed and now must lie on it.
I've decided to try once more.
I'm not completely sure of this;
His behaviour was so poor.

I've burnt my boat and told the world
That we are on again,
So now I only need to prove
I won't break up from the strain.

So why go back for more,
If it all was so terribly dire?
But life wasn't always a bore,
And there was a lot to inspire.

There has always been
An underlying love, kept alive.
We returned again and again,
As if we needed the other to survive.

Our happiness at stake now,
I see in this a rescue scheme.
He doesn't like being alone;
Nor do I, it seems.

I'll be trying very hard
To control the situation;
I'll be the one in charge
Of a covert manipulation.

This project requires management:
If I fail, the penalty's high for me.
It will be a return to loneliness,
An unpalatable predicament.

We're risking a lot with this move;
At stake is a life sentence of loneliness,
But more importantly, for both of us,
Love's labours lost indeed.

Silenced

I am silenced now,
My voice unheard,
My thoughts unknown,
My face sombre.

Frozen out of speech
By speech spoken over,
Disallowed, expounding—
No answers to queries.

What could I have said
Or done
When I am unable to say
Or do,
My sins as unknown
As the reason behind the ice?

I am silenced now
By the silence of another ...

Part-Time Marriage

All the time we've been married,
We've shared our time—
Half of it at your home,
The other part alone.

It was such a shock to find,
Despite the longings of our hearts
And dictates of society,
We were happier living apart.

I have a secret second life
When I'm not with you;
I've turned into a part-time wife
With a part-time love for you.

Of course, you have your secret life;
You think it's safe from me,
But as with every other wife,
Your secrets are not that to me.

But things have changed,
And as have we, and for a start,
We spend half our time at my home,
The other half apart.

Though I hated your home,
Your hatred of mine is more;
I find myself a part-time wife,
Seeing less of you than before!

What Is Love but a Heartache?

Love always breaks your heart,
Or so the songs always say;
And then we always get to the part
Where they go their separate ways,
While our forlorn singer declares underlying love
To the betrayer, singing of love
Through tears of despair,
As though love triumphs over all—

As the songs always say.

But just like in the movies, reality intrudes,
Crudely and forcefully revealing the brutality
That tarnishes the gold shine of the dream,
And brings with it the clatter and clanging of reality,
Because love in real life is not real.
It is merely an idea, a construction,
Like a song or a movie—a pretence, a lie.
Love only triumphs in our imagination—

As the movies always show.

The reality of life transcends desire.
Love is a concept, an idea,
Something to which we can aspire
Only so because of chemistry—
A hormone cocktail cleverly contrived
By nature in its eternal unceasing desire
To continue its only objective:
To ensure we continue to survive—

As life always demonstrates.

So what is love but a heartache,
When there is no such thing as love?
There is no pill we can take
That would stop the chemical rush,
And there is no way we can make
It all go away without more of the same.
So losing love is a heartache.
It is all just nature's game—

Or so the songs should say.

I Dreamt of You Again Last Night

I dreamt of you again last night.
I saw you standing there
Against the night—
Not a shred of light
To show your face.
But I know your smell,
The very shape of your head,
And that gleam of your eye,
And I cried and cried
In grief at your loss—
To think that I'll never see you
Standing there against the night.

I mourn your loss every day;
Every day, I think of the way
You walked away from me.
Such words we said,
Words only said in dread:
Full of portent, full of threat!
If only they could all be unsaid!
I could rake back every word
And make every word unheard
And see you really standing there.

I dreamt of you again last night.
I saw you standing there
Against the light.
Oh, that I might see you again.
I would ask you then
To come and share my dreams.

Speak Not of Love

Speak not of love;
It does not endure.
Do not talk of love;
Love so often dies.
Do not give of love;
Love so often lies.

Love does not stay;
It does not last.
And day by day,
As time goes past,
Love fades away;
Love never lasts.

Don't give of love;
It always takes
And never returns.
Don't give your love;
It always makes
A fool of you.

Don't talk of love;
It doesn't last,
It isn't real.
Don't think of love;
Give love a miss—
And always be free.

Often I Sit and Muse on the Nature of Love

Often I sit and muse on the nature of love
And my role in the scheme of things;
Of love and lovers and dear ones too,
Those too close to bear to lose;

Of parents to whom all respect
Is due and brothers who over time
Grow distant with passing age,
Their lives a pale copy of former climes;

Of children, those fruit of my loins,
And those of theirs, those precious coins,
These tokens of love whose lives become
Treasure to me in my immortality.

But am I that only—a mother, a grandam,
Sitting and sewing and advising those ones
Who make the same mistakes,
Love the same, feel the same way?

I have loved too much in my way—
Lust that died far too soon,
Passion that withered like a leaf
In autumn, drying and browning.

Love left me sour, dried, regretful,
Wanting to leave, needing to go,
Trying to find a way
From a coming winter of loneliness.

For more is needed; more is wanted.
Life is empty when love is spent.
Life needs love to feel alive.
Life's not lived when love has died.

But I remember, then, that I cannot go.
Those children, those calls on my life,
Who are all of life to me
Need my life for theirs to grow.

Is that all I am—a grandmother
Sitting and sewing and advising,
Warning against missteps, mischance,
Caring for and minding the young?

For love is many things:
Agape, philia, eros, and
Even storge, philautia.[16]
Each has a place in the grand scheme;

But is my place, my role, my duty
To sit and sew and advise the young,
Growing old and dry and passionless,
Dry and lonely within a crowd?

---

[16] The following are types of love: *agape* (love for everyone), *philia* (deep friendship), *eros* (sexual love), *storge* (fondness of association, such as family), and *philautia* (love of the self).

For all my age, I am young at heart,
Willing Eros to mark me with his little dart
And give me that which I thought had gone,
Along with youth and relentless time,

For time is the enemy in all these things.
Love grows and wanes with time.
Time changes those whose love is best,
As time changes those who are left.

Eros comes and goes, passion and lust,
Time not dimming or changing need;
All is there for someone to come
And pick up on the continuing need.

And if indeed Eros' dart struck
And gave me back my youth again,
Would love make me young once more,
Turning back time's relentlessness?

No, love won't stop time,
But time stops with love, pauses.
Time passes in another realm;
Love conquers everything.

For love is needed, required;
Even for an advising grandsire,
The matriarch sitting and advising
Wants eros as well as agape, philia.

Love in all its forms, all its ways,
Lives in all of us, all our days,
The need not dying with passing time—
Indeed, time passing the only crime.

For love is powerful and must,
Like time, pass from stage to stage.
Like time, it has seasons that grow and wane.
Love changes as time progresses.

But of all that time has checked,
Eros is the one that time has bid
Good night; with age comes loneliness.
Eros is youth, and youth won't stay.

For all the talk of love, in all its forms—
Agape and philia and eros—
Eros is mostly invited to play,
Even when he won't deign to stay.

Printed in the United States
By Bookmasters